Turning

Green

By Barbara Rudow

Scobre Press Corporation
2255 Calle Clara
La Jolla, CA 92037

Scobre Press books may be purchased for
educational, business or sales promotional use.
First Scobre edition published 2008.

Edited by Charlotte Graeber
Cover Art & Layout by Michael Lynch

ISBN # 1-934713-24-4

TOUCHDOWN EDITION
This story is based on the real life of Jessica
Assaf, although some names, quotes, and details
of events have been altered.

CHAPTER ONE

GREEN'S THE NEW PINK

"Green is the new pink." That's a pretty catchy phrase, isn't it?

Basically, it means that caring about the environment is a growing trend. From movie stars, to politicians, to the family next door, it seems like everyone is "going green" … and for the sake of our planet, we have to hope that it's not just the newest fad.

What does it mean to be green? Well, green is the symbolic color of environmentalism. Living green means understanding that your actions have an effect on the environment—and then, with that information in hand, trying to live your life in a way that does as little damage as possible to the Earth. The simple choices all of us make every day are a big part of that.

Going green is a really important job because the stakes are so high: We have to save the world! Our planet is in great danger. We are facing threats in our air, in our water, on our land, and in the products we use every day. And not only is the Earth at risk, but every one of us is also personally under attack. The scary fact is that many of the products we use and the foods we eat every day are harmful to us *and* the environment.

So, are *you* living green?

There are a lot of questions you can ask yourself to help figure it out: Do you use products that are made with all-natural ingredients? Do you frequently ride in gas-guzzling cars? Do you eat organic foods? Do you wear clothes that, when they're produced, emit harmful pollutants into the environment? Do you leave the water running while brushing your teeth? Do you recycle as much as possible? Do you leave lights on when you are not using them? Do you wear makeup that is harmful to the environment— and even your own face?

Most of us have mixed answers to these questions—some good, some bad. The trick is acting on your answers—and making some simple but possibly world-saving changes in your own life. From morning until night, every day, you make hundreds of choices that affect the environment. We all do. Together, if we make the right choices in being eco-friendly, we can make a big difference.

When former vice president and Nobel Peace Prize winner Al Gore started talking about global warming a few years ago, many people didn't want to listen. (Global warming is a fancy way of saying that our planet is heating up.) The title of Mr. Gore's documentary on global warming sums up the situation well: "An Inconvenient Truth."

Sure, it's easier to believe that there is no problem, or that someone else will take care of it. But the *inconvenient* truth is that global warming, and other environmental issues, affect all of us. After all, there is only one planet Earth.

The reason that global warming is happening is because of a process known as the "greenhouse effect." This natural phenomenon gets its name from the way a greenhouse (a glass building plants are grown in) works.

Have you ever sat in a car with the windows rolled up on a sunny day? It gets hot in the car pretty fast, right? Well, that's how a greenhouse works, too. Heat from the sun passes through the glass and warms up the ground inside the greenhouse (or the seats inside your car), which heats up the air above it. The warm air is trapped inside, keeping the greenhouse warm enough to grow plants all year long, even in places with really cold winters.

The greenhouse effect that's happening to our planet is a similar process. Certain gases in our atmosphere trap energy from the sun, called radiation. (These gases act like the glass in a green-house, and we call them greenhouse gases. They include carbon dioxide, methane, and nitrous oxide.)

This energy from the sun is what warms the Earth, so having *some* amount of these gases is actually good for the Earth's temperature. In fact, if these gases weren't there at all, the sun's radiation would bounce off the Earth and just go right back into space, making the Earth too cold for us to live on.

But now, we have way too much of these gases in our atmosphere. This is because over the last couple hundred years, humans have begun to build things that produce these gases as part of how they work. Cars, airplanes, power plants, and factories that make the products we use every day all give off greenhouse gases.

And that's not all—there's also a lot more of us humans now than there were even a few hundred years ago. That means more cars to drive us all around and more factories to make all the stuff we need. Add it all up, and those extra greenhouse gases are trapping a lot more of the sun's radiation than our atmosphere used to. As a result, our planet is heating up: global warming.

Global warming affects more than just the temperatures around us, however. It can also change weather patterns. For example, warmer ocean water tends to produce bigger storms. We have recently seen the results of this phenomenon in the United States with powerful hurricanes like Katrina, Rita, and Wilma.

Our oceans are at the center of other frightening climate trends as well. In recent years, as oceans have become warmer, water levels have risen. This may be because, as the water warms due to global warming, the ice near the North and South Poles begins to melt, adding more water to the ocean. These deposits of ice, which are called the polar ice caps, are enormous. When chunks of them start to melt and collapse into the ocean, they can quickly disappear. Think of an ice cube in a glass of water—it will melt a lot faster if there are fewer ice cubes surrounding it.

In 2002, a giant chunk of ice (about 1,300 square miles in size, weighing 720 billion tons) collapsed into the ocean. This ice was said to have been stable for the past 12,000 years before breaking off! Some scientists fear that if warming continues, more and more of these giant chunks of ice will break off and melt into the ocean. If they do, many coastal areas will be flooded. This could be devastating to coastlines in states like Florida and California, and entire countries like Japan. If enough of the polar ice caps melt, millions of people living in coastal areas around the world could lose their homes, or worse—entire cities could be destroyed.

As the polar ice caps melt, polar bears like this one find it harder to survive. In fact, researchers were startled to find polar bears having to swim up to 60 miles across open sea to find food and a place to rest. Many are drowning or starving to death because of it.

Some of the side effects of rising temperatures are less obvious than others. That's because they are occurring *below* the surface of the ocean. Global warming is causing the destruction of thousands of miles of coral reefs, and we must protect them.

Coral reefs have often been referred to as "tropical rainforests of the ocean" because of the great number of plant and animal species they support. Reefs protect our shorelines, and are a key part of our oceans' food chain. In one year (1998), 16 percent of the world's reefs were lost!

Can you imagine if we lose our reefs and beaches altogether? What would the side effects be on the rest of nature?

Despite the scary trends we are witnessing, there is some good news. We can help the coral reefs recover; we can stop the Earth from warming; we can help keep storms from growing stronger; and we can take control of the chemicals we put into our bodies, our water, and our air. In other words, we can save our planet if we each do our part!

There is no simple fix, however. It took the whole world to get us into this mess, and it will take every one of us to get us out. We've spent the last few hundred years turning the world into a polluted mess. Now we have to spend the next few hundred turning it green again.

Millions of individuals have already begun to do their part, and environmental groups from around the world have worked hard to spread the word. There are thousands of initiatives being put into effect by governments and organizations all over the world, from London to San Francisco to Tokyo to Vancouver. They include recycling projects, clean-air acts, the distribution of information about which consumer products are safe and which aren't, and many other small steps toward saving planet Earth.

The Kyoto Protocol was the first real effort to begin reducing the production of greenhouse gases on a *global* scale. The Kyoto Protocol got its name because it was adopted at a United Nations meeting in Kyoto, Japan, in 1997.

(It is actually an update to a treaty first created by the United Nations in 1992. That first treaty said that the world needed to reduce greenhouse gases. But it didn't set any limits on individual countries, and it didn't give the United Nations any way to enforce the rules. That's what makes the Kyoto Protocol so important—it is a much tougher set of rules.)

Since 1997, 182 countries have agreed to the protocol, promising to monitor and reduce their own greenhouse gas emissions. (The United States has not yet agreed to the protocol.)

In addition to environmentalists and politicians, several celebrities have been key proponents of the green movement. They are using their exposure to help people understand that "going green" is more than just talk. Leonardo DiCaprio is one of the celebrities leading the way. In addition to producing the documentary "The 11th Hour," he has also encouraged many celebrities to skip the limousines at the Oscars and arrive in hybrid cars instead.

GREEN FACT: Hybrid cars use about half the gas regular cars do, and they spit out 89 percent fewer harmful emissions. So when you drive a hybrid, fewer greenhouse gases are going into our atmosphere. Of course, when you walk or ride a bike, NO harmful chemicals are emitted!

Cameron Diaz and Chevy Chase were just two of the celebrities that readily joined in. Sheryl Crow went a step further and actually toured the country in a bus that was powered by vegetable oil. Fuel made from vegetable oils is called "biodiesel," and it can be produced from leftover oil collected from fast food restaurants like McDonald's. Crow thought her eco-friendly bus was fun to ride in, even though she said it smelled like french fries the entire way! Other celebrities like George Clooney, Ed Norton, Robert Redford, Cate Blanchett, and Tom Hanks are also doing their part to raise money and awareness for the green movement.

Sure, these are small steps. But when you multiply these small steps several *billion* times, they really add up. To turn the world green again, millions and millions of non-politicians and non-celebrities will have to do their part as well.

In the following pages, you'll read about how the actions of young people, such as 17-year-old Jessica Assaf, can make a huge difference in saving the planet. For Jessica, becoming an active part of the green movement was personal and unexpected. After learning about some environmentally questionable practices occurring in the makeup industry, she stood up for herself … and for planet Earth.

CHAPTER TWO

ONE PERSON MAKES A DIFFERENCE

Jessica Assaf started attending The Branson School, a high school in Northern California, in 2003. One of the requirements to graduate from Branson is that each student has to complete a certain number of community service hours each year. Because of her interest in the environment, Jessica was drawn to a local initiative known as "Teens for Safe Cosmetics" to fulfill her community service requirement.

Jessica had been wearing makeup since she was 13, so the topic was definitely interesting to her. Still, she was unsure about what the group was all about. She was well aware that makeup is used by millions of people every day— but didn't understand how it could possibly be unsafe to people and the environment. Didn't the companies who make the makeup care about the health of the people who wore it? Didn't they feel responsible to keep the world free of harmful pollutants? Hadn't they ever heard of global warming? Wasn't *somebody* monitoring them and making sure that their ingredients weren't bad for people? The more answers Jessica found to these questions, the more disturbed she became.

Like millions of other teenagers, Jessica started to wear lip gloss and nail polish at about the age of 12. She and her friends later started experimenting with other makeup by doing makeovers on each other. They practiced with eye shadow, blush, lipstick, eyeliner, and mascara. Most of their makeup choices were made based on what they read in magazines and saw on TV. By high school, putting on makeup was part of their daily routines—like brushing their teeth or eating breakfast.

Toxic?

Not once did Jessica think about the harmful effects the chemicals used in producing makeup were having on the environment. And not once did she turn a box of makeup over to read the ingredients she was putting on her own face. Even if she had, they wouldn't have meant anything to her. The jumble of scientific names might as well have been written in a foreign language. To Jessica and most girls, makeup was pure fun—they didn't give it any thought beyond what they saw in the mirror.

That's why her first meeting with Judi Shils, the founder of Teens for Safe Cosmetics, wasn't something she was taking too seriously. Being a part of this group just sounded like a fun way to fill her graduation requirement. Jessica had no idea that this meeting would change her life.

The meeting took place at Branson High. Jessica and three other high school girls attended, along with Judi Shils and a chemist who had worked for several major cosmetics companies. The chemist spoke to the group about all the harmful ingredients contained in the cosmetics that millions of people were using every day. After he had spoken for about five minutes, the girls were totally floored.

They soon found out that many of the products they were using were harmful to them *and* the environment. The ingredients included a long list of toxic chemicals that were linked to cancer, birth defects, reproductive disorders, and many other health-related problems. These poisonous chemicals were in the products they used every day—and nobody ever told them! To make matters worse, they were manufactured and disposed of with little regard for the environment, so even people who didn't wear makeup suffered.

Jessica was astonished. *Why didn't people know about this?* she wondered. In an instant, Jessica went from being totally confused to totally upset. And then she went from the room they were sitting in to the bathroom, where she proceeded to wash all of the makeup from her face.

When she returned, the chemist began talking about a major makeup company that he had once worked for. Jessica asked if he thought the owners of the company used their own products. The answer made her cringe. Not only did they not use them, he said, they thought they were junk.

The second thing that alarmed Jessica was when she found out that cosmetics are not regulated by the U.S. Food and Drug Administration (or FDA for short). The FDA is the federal government agency that is responsible for making sure the food you eat, and the products you use, are safe. They inspect, test, and set standards for products that are made and sold in the United States.

The FDA is largely responsible for food providers listing nutritional information. To be healthy, people need to know what they are putting into their bodies. Shouldn't the makeup industry have to do the same thing? After all, these products are used on people's faces ... every day!

Unlike most other products, cosmetics do *not* have to be approved by the FDA before they are sold. That means that companies can use any ingredients they want in their products, even if they are harmful to people and the environment.

This information got Jessica so fired up that she decided to take immediate action. After leaving that meeting with the chemist (with a list of harmful chemicals in hand), Jessica went straight home to check the ingredients that were in *her* makeup products.

GREEN INFO: www.cosmeticsdatabase.com is a great website for checking the ingredients in your makeup and personal care products.

She quickly discovered that almost all of the products she used contained potentially harmful ingredients. Totally disgusted, Jessica grabbed all of her makeup and tossed it into a big black trash bag. This was a huge deal because Jessica loved makeup and had invested a lot of money in her collection of products. The truth was, she didn't want to stop wearing makeup altogether. Instead, she became determined to find products that both looked good and were safe to use. She saw no reason to risk her health over nail polish or mascara—especially, because she could get the same look from safer products!

What makeup *is* safe to use and not harmful to the environment? That is one of the questions that Teens for Safe Cosmetics (also referred to as TSC) and the national Campaign for Safe Cosmetics are helping to answer. Teens for Safe Cosmetics, a local coalition in Northern California, works closely with the national safe cosmetics campaign. The two groups have similar goals: First, they want to educate the public about the potentially toxic ingredients in the makeup and personal care products that people use every day (mascara, soap, deodorant, lotion, etc.). Both groups also try to spread information to the public about the existence of "green" alternatives, which are environmentally friendly versions.

The girls from TSC learn more about potentially toxic ingredients during a presentation.

After a short time, Jessica became very passionate about TSC's cause. Still, she preferred to stay in her comfort zone, which was on the sidelines. Jessica had always been very shy and didn't like to be the center of attention. But her strong belief that people needed to know the truth about the products they were using changed all that. Through her many experiences with TSC, Jessica became more and more comfortable speaking in public. In fact, she eventually became the main spokesperson for TSC and the driving force behind the movement.

Jessica's public speaking career kicked off when she was a 14-year-old freshman. Although she was very uncomfortable, she bravely committed to doing a presentation in front of the entire school. After becoming so passionate about environmentalism (and safe cosmetics, in particular), she felt that she simply *had* to share her knowledge. Despite her enthusiasm, she was scared to death!

It's every teen's worst nightmare to do something embarrassing in front of the entire school—and of course, Jessica did just that. With the entire school watching her, Jessica carefully walked up the steps and onto the stage.

Just as she hit the second to last step, she tripped and fell to the ground, face first with a thud. Laughter rippled through the auditorium, and Jessica turned cherry red. In that moment, all she wanted to do was crawl away and hide. Instead, she stood up and bravely kept walking toward the podium.

The next obstacle she had to overcome came from her computer. For some reason, her PowerPoint presentation wasn't working right. *What next?* she wondered. While everyone waited— still giddy from watching Jessica take a tumble a few seconds earlier—she finally got her presentation to work. Then she took a deep breath and proceeded.

The main message Jessica put out that day was to tell the audience that they could each make a difference in saving the planet, and themselves. Her main point was that since everybody uses personal care products, this was a really simple place to start. "Toxic chemicals are not only harmful to our bodies—they are harmful to our environment. By taking some small steps to make ourselves healthier, we are also helping our planet," she said at the beginning of her speech. "It's a no-brainer."

Then she went on, challenging her classmates to think about how the toxic chemicals in the products they use are processed and disposed of. She showed them charts and statistics, and even handed out fliers with lists of dangerous chemicals they could look out for. "Do you really want to support companies that are polluting the Earth?" she asked. "Do you really want to put these disgusting toxins on your body?"

Look through *your* medicine cabinet today! Many of the products you use may be toxic. Then, check out the index of this book to find a list of "greener alternatives." Why put harmful chemicals on your body?

Jessica's passion for her subject was evident, but still, she could tell that many of her classmates remained unconvinced. Some were interested in learning more, but others thought she was making too big of a deal out of something as superficial as makeup. Jessica was not about to give up, though.

"This issue is not just about changing lipstick and deodorant," she told them. "It's about social justice." The more she spoke, the more engaged the audience became. She could tell that they were starting to get it. When she ended her speech, her voice rose, and she became even more passionate. "Putting poisonous chemicals in our makeup without telling us is a violation of our trust. As consumers, we expect that we are buying products that are safe. If that is not the case, don't we have a right to know?"

TSC believes that people *do* have a right to know, so they came up with a list of the most toxic chemicals in the makeup commonly used by teens. This list is known as the "Dirty Dozen +" (see index).

To create this list, TSC surveyed over 500 teens. They discovered that most of them used about 10-20 personal care products per day. They also found that many of the teenagers were using the same brands. They took the most popular items from that list and researched the ingredients in each product (with the help of their chemist friends, of course).

The list they created made them sick. They found toxic chemicals in almost every product. There was some stuff that was just plain gross. For example, they found out that one of the ingredients in popular mascaras is also used to clean airplane wheels. (The people who touch the wheels wear gloves to protect their hands from it!) Do you really want that stuff near your eyes?

Of course, this group of crusaders knew that people, including themselves, were not going to just stop using their favorite products. TSC had to let people know about alternatives to switch over to, so they came up with a list of "safe" companies. These are companies that use "green alternatives" to make great products. This list, titled "Greener Alternatives" (see index), was printed on the back of the flier for the Dirty Dozen.

Green makeup looks the same as regular makeup, although it tends to be lighter

The Dirty Dozen fliers were first handed out when "Operation Beauty Drop" was launched. Operation Beauty Drop was TSC's first "action." TSC decided to organize at least one action each month to spread the word about safe and unsafe products. For this event, they decorated drop-boxes and put them at high-profile places (like malls and supermarkets). People dropped off their empty makeup and product containers, and they received a flier with the Dirty Dozen and Greener Alternatives lists.

Operation Beauty Drop helped the team find out what products were being used, while also educating the public about those products. To get people to come by, the team created posters, flyers, and a giant face using the empty containers and the Dirty Dozen list. It was hard to miss, which was exactly what they wanted—but was it enough?

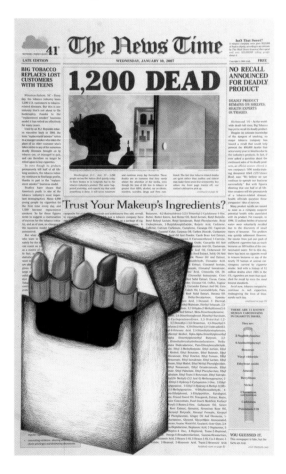

21

CHAPTER THREE

GREEN GLITZ AND GLAM

Teens love music, so TSC cleverly chose to have a "Battle of the Bands" as the entertainment for their next event. Their hope, as always, was to get their message out to as many people as possible. This event was held at the local teen center. Ten bands were selected to compete, and each band was asked to play one set. Local celebrities and teachers acted as judges. The first place winner would get the opportunity to use a recording studio for an entire day, which enticed a lot of up-and-coming bands to participate. The price of admission for the general public was used to help fund TSC so they could continue their campaign.

Hundreds of teens came, both to enjoy the music and to learn about green products. In between sets, Jessica and other members of TSC spoke about their campaign for a few minutes. They told the teen audience how they could get involved in projects like this one, projects that strive to improve the way we live. Jessica was still a bit nervous speaking in public, but she was gaining confidence with each presentation.

Jessica was interviewed by a local radio station prior to a TSC event in 2007.

The Battle of the Bands was so successful that when the next event was scheduled, music was incorporated again. This event was called the "Green Glitz and Glam Benefit Ball," and it was held at Jessica's high school. About 350 people attended, which was a huge turnout! The event included a fashion show, dinner, and dance.

Jessica was extra-excited about this event because it reached beyond safe cosmetics. TSC wanted people to know that "going green" was a positive thing that could be incorporated into all areas of a person's life, not just through personal care products. The girls talked about the environment, global warming, green product alternatives, and simple steps that teens could take to change the world for the better.

A cool component of this event was the runway they set up. TSC searched for companies who were creating green fashion. The one rule was that the fashion on the runway had to come from companies using only organic and sustainable products. They also had to be environmentally conscious in their manufacturing, and not be involved in any unfair treatment of their labor. In other words, they wanted to find companies that stood for all the right things.

The words "organic" and "sustainability" are used a lot today, but what do they mean? The dictionary definition of sustainable is "capable of being continued with minimal long-term effect on the environment." Sustainable companies meet the needs of their company today, without compromising the ability of future generations to meet their own needs.

Fortunately, there are many companies who have already "gone green." Clif Bar Inc. is a good example (www.clifbar.com). The company uses recycled packaging, organic ingredients, and recycled paperboard for the containers that hold their nutrition bars. The recycled paperboard alone is expected to save an estimated 7,500 trees and an estimated 3.3 million gallons of water each year. How awesome is that? Think about how it would impact our world if every company did that!

The word "organic" does not need to be scary. Organic clothing doesn't look any different than non-organic clothing. It is simply healthier for people and the environment. The difference is in how the item is grown and manufactured. Organic materials are grown without the use of chemicals. The manufacturing process also uses organic products and is eco-friendly.

Non-organic clothing (which is most of the clothing available at major stores) starts out in fields covered in pesticides. These chemicals may stay in the material and eventually end up on your body. Think about this: A simple cotton T-shirt that is non-organic can take up to one-third of a pound of chemicals to make! Not only are consumers being exposed to those chemicals, but it is estimated that about 20,000 farm workers die every year in developing countries from pesticide poisoning. Many of these deaths come from cotton farming.

Many stages of popular manufacturing processes use harmful chemicals (from chlorine to polyvinyl). And the toxic chemicals that you don't end up wearing often become waste that manufacturers have to dispose of. A lot of these chemicals eventually end up seeping into our rivers, lakes, and even our drinking water. Gross!

Thirsty?

TSC wanted no part of that. At the fashion show, TSC proudly displayed all-organic clothing, makeup, and accessories—and they were amazing! Many of the featured fashions at the Green Glitz and Glam Benefit Ball were provided by Stewart+Brown, a company that specializes in organic clothing. Local teens and merchants also made some of the clothes using organic fabric. There were even prom dresses made using organic silk!

The food for the Green Glitz and Glam Benefit Ball was donated from some of the best restaurants in Northern California—and once again, everything was organic. The dinner included organic pasta, organic salad, and even organic pizza.

GREEN FACT: Foods can only be labeled "organic" if they meet the standards set by the U.S. Department of Agriculture (USDA). If a product is labeled "organic," it means that a certified government worker inspected the farm where it was grown to make sure that the growers followed all the rules to meet the USDA organic standards. The farmers must use sustainable farming methods, meaning that they don't hurt the environment. This includes preserving agricultural land and treating animals fairly.

After the all-organic dinner, the Green Glitz and Glam Benefit Ball moved on to the fashion show. The TSC girls, with help from some volunteers, did a great job decorating the gymnasium where the event took place. They covered the walls in organic fabric and situated elegantly draped tables around the runway so that everybody could enjoy the show.

The fashion show took the audience on a diverse journey into green fashion. The models displayed sustainable clothing for all occasions, from casual and formal attire to sleepwear. The models were all local teens, too—which was a cool touch. Because the prom was only a few months away, the organic prom dresses on display were a huge hit. The jewelry that went with the dresses (made from recycled materials) also received major attention. But Jessica thinks it was the makeup the models wore (produced from the Greener Alternatives list) that made the biggest splash.

Jessica and another TSC member, Heather, were the emcees (or hosts) for the evening. Other members of the campaign were models and dressers backstage. Even Jessica's family got involved. Her two teenage brothers filmed the entire evening. Although they used to tease Jessica about her campaign, they were starting to appreciate what their sister was trying to do.

Jessica, her two brothers, and her sister.

By "turning green" with your clothing and products, you don't have to completely change your look, only some of your lifestyle choices. And you are making an important statement: "I care about what happens to the planet."

This is TSC's message. Although it started with cosmetics, they don't want people to just change their lipstick and nail polish. They want people to make informed decisions about *all* the products they choose, from makeup to clothing to food.

Judi Shils, leader of TSC, says, "We hope it's a starting point. If people are mindful about what they put *on* their body, they'll be mindful about what they put *in* their body." Remember, urning green has no limits—you just keep on turning!

CHAPTER FOUR

SACRAMENTO, HERE WE COME

In 2005, TSC was contacted by California State Senator Carole Migden, who had heard about the work the group was doing. The senator was trying to pass a bill called the California Safe Cosmetics Act of 2005, and thought the group might be able to help.

The California Safe Cosmetics Act, if passed into law, would require the manufacturers of all cosmetics and body-care products to list all the ingredients in their products, especially those known or suspected to cause cancer, birth defects, or other reproductive harm. The list would go to the California Department of Public Health and be available to all consumers. This would be a big step in the fight for safer cosmetics, as people could actually find out what was in the products they were using.

But taking on a billion-dollar industry was definitely going to be an uphill battle. The cosmetics companies were fighting hard against the passage of this bill, because it was going to cost them extra money—and potentially expose their unsafe practices to the public!

TSC agreed to help Senator Migden, and the girls quickly sprung into action. Jessica had never done anything like this before. She recalled history lessons about the state government, but she never dreamed that she would actually become involved.

The California State Legislature is made up of two houses: the Senate and Assembly. There are 40 senators and 80 assembly members. Together, they represent the people of California.

Jessica knew that the passage of this bill would be very significant. After all, more than 35 million people live in sunny California. Beyond that, the passage of this bill would have a huge impact on every American who buys cosmetics.

The first step toward getting a bill passed is to have a senator or assembly member decide to "author" a bill (meaning, he or she is the person in charge of getting it passed). In this case, Senator Migden had already agreed to author the California Safe Cosmetics Act.

The next step is to present the idea to the Office of the Legislative Counsel so it can be drafted into bill form. After that, the bill is introduced and is assigned to a policy committee for review. During this review, testimony can be heard in support of, or opposition to, the bill. The bill can be passed, defeated, or amended.

Since Carole Migden was the author, and a state senator, her bill would first be presented to the Senate, then to the Assembly. The bill would be carefully reviewed before being put to a vote. If both houses passed the bill, it would be sent to the governor, who would then have three choices: sign it into law, allow it to become a law without his signature, or veto it. (A veto would mean that the bill is squashed.) On the other hand, if it is approved, it then becomes part of the California Codes, which are a complete collection of laws used to govern the state.

When Senator Migden contacted TSC, the California Safe Cosmetics Act (also known as Senate Bill 484, or SB 484 for short) was about to be presented to the Senate. She did not expect it to pass. But TSC was determined to give it a fighting chance.

The first thing TSC decided to do was go to Sacramento, California's state capital, to lobby (voice their support) for the bill. Judi Shils and five members of TSC drove one and a half hours to Sacramento. They carried signs declaring their cause, and spoke with anybody who would listen.

None of the TSC members had ever done anything like

this before, so they wisely hired a lobbyist to show them the ropes. A lobbyist is a person who tries to influence public officials to take certain actions—in this case, to vote for the California Safe Cosmetics Act (SB 484).

The lobbyist who helped them, Mr. Pete Price, was awesome. He taught them how the process worked and how to approach the politicians. He even went into the meetings with them to help present their case.

Their mission on this first visit was simply to explain what SB 484 was, and why it was important. They were able to talk with several state legislators, but they knew they would have to contact many more if they were going to influence this bill. Before heading home, they scheduled future meetings with everyone they could.

Jessica and several members of TSC prepare for their meetings in Sacramento.

The group made a second trip to Sacramento the following week. They spent the entire day at the Capitol building in meetings, desperately trying to get people to understand the importance of this issue. The bill would be the first step in holding companies responsible for their products, and giving consumers the ability to make safe choices. How could people decide what products were and were not safe if they had no idea what was in them?

Through their research, Jessica and her group discovered that in Europe, because of the European Cosmetics Directive, more than 1,100 chemical substances had been *banned* for use in cosmetics. In the United States, only nine of these substances had been banned! The other 1,091 were still being used, despite being eliminated from similar products in Europe for years. Examples are ingredients such as coal tar, which is used in shampoo, and petrolatum, which is used to make lipstick shine.

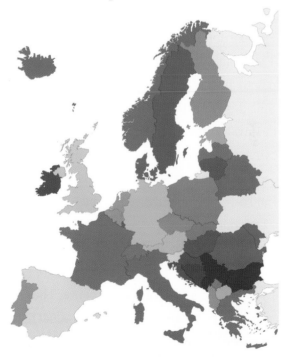

If all of the countries in Europe have banned these chemicals, how come we are still using them?

Why are harmful chemicals allowed here in the United States when they are considered too dangerous for people to use in Europe? Jessica asked that question to any senator who would listen.

What Jessica ultimately discovered was that most companies play by the rules they are given. Since they are not *required* by law to list their ingredients, they don't. Clearly, it was time to change the rules. If the companies wouldn't do the right thing on their own, then a law needed to go into effect that would *require* them to make safer products. SB 484 would help to do just that.

Although the members of TSC were only teenagers, they quickly realized that they could actually make a difference! As it turned out, the fact that they were so young probably worked to their advantage. The politicians had to listen to adults all the time, so seeing a group of girls who were so passionate about their cause made them take notice.

TSC's hard work paid off: With their support, SB 484 passed in both the Senate and the Assembly!

Still, despite all their efforts, the bill was not expected to be signed into law by Governor Arnold Schwarzenegger. In fact, the cosmetics industry spent millions of dollars to make sure it wouldn't be. They sent out hundreds of gift bags filled with free cosmetics to senators and assembly members, and spent tons of money lobbying against this bill.

Their position on why the bill shouldn't be passed was simple: It was going to cost them more money for no reason, they said. They saw it as an unnecessary expense. They said that they were able to get a consistent, affordable product that worked for the general public by using the chemicals they'd always used. Many of the cosmetics companies insisted that the amount of chemicals in their products was too small to be dangerous. Listing them would only cause an unnecessary panic, they claimed.

But how could they know that for sure when many chemists were saying the exact opposite? Was that a risk worth taking? Jessica didn't think so.

Although there is not yet definitive proof that these chemicals directly cause cancer and other health-related problems, there is also no proof that the combination of them is not dangerous. In fact, many studies have been done recently to suggest that the "cocktail" of chemicals we put into our bodies daily is, in fact, very dangerous.

Scientist have a pretty good idea about which chemicals are safe and which are dangerous. But there is little known about the results of mixing chemicals together over a long period of time in "chemical cocktails."

Whether or not you believe these chemicals are unsafe, shouldn't it be *your choice* as to what goes on your body, and not the cosmetics industry's choice? (Remember, many of the people making this choice don't even use their own products!)

This legislative process was both exhilarating and frustrating for Jessica. She was proud of what they were doing, but sometimes felt as if they weren't making progress. TSC could not compete with the cosmetics industry on a financial level, and they had exhausted all their other resources.

Jessica was not about to give up, though—they had come too far. So, Jessica, Judi Shils, and several members of their team decided to make one last effort. They piled into the car and headed to Sacramento one more time, determined to meet with Governor Schwarzenegger himself.

When they got to the Capitol, they camped outside the governor's office and waited. They held their signs high in the air, and as Jessica says, "spoke to anybody who looked important." They had been sitting for over two hours when they were told that the governor was out of the state and there was no way they could see him. It appeared as though they had trav

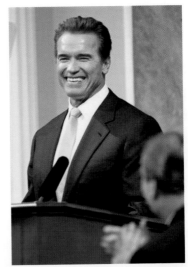

Governor Schwarzenegger

eled all this way only to be shot down. Jessica wanted to cry. Instead, she went into action.

The governor is a busy person, so every bill that comes before him is assigned to an analyst. The analyst does all the research regarding the issue, then makes a recommendation to the governor about whether the bill should pass or not. Jessica knew that if they could speak with the analyst, they might still have a shot at getting the bill passed.

Jessica saw a man come out of the governor's office, and she told him that she desperately needed to speak with the analyst assigned to the California Safe Cosmetics Act. The man was nice, and told the girls he would see what he could do. Then he disappeared back into the office.

Outside on the bench, the nervous girls held hands. It all came down to this. To their surprise, their wish was granted: The man got them a meeting with the analyst assigned to SB 484! When the analyst let them into her office, she abruptly said, "You each have five minutes."

The girls scurried into the conference room and sat around a giant oval table. Jessica couldn't stop her hands from sweating. This was the state government, and she was only a 17-year-old—it was very intimidating!

Since each girl only had five minutes to speak, they tried to highlight different reasons why the bill should be passed. When it was her turn, Jessica pushed her fears aside and began a passionate plea for every person's right to make informed decisions. Jessica astutely argued that the companies should be required to list the ingredients so that people could decide for themselves which risks they did and didn't want to take.

The high school junior went on to explain that most people use 10 to 20 personal care products on a daily basis, which means they are exposed to about 200 chemicals every day. Some of these chemicals may only be present in trace amounts. But there is no definitive research exploring what the combinations of these chemicals do to our bodies with prolonged use.

Furthermore, most people assume that the products they use are regulated by the FDA, so they use them without thinking. The truth is that they aren't. Only 11 percent of 6,500 products on the market have been checked by the FDA. Listing the ingredients is a simple and logical step—and one that every person has the right to.

In the middle of Jessica's five minutes, the analyst started asking questions. This made it difficult for Jessica to know if her message was being well-received. But at least she knew that the analyst was taking her seriously. The analyst was concerned about how much money the companies would lose if the bill was passed. Instead of cowering at this question, Jessica argued that it wasn't relevant. After all, sacrificing a person's health for profit didn't make much sense, Jessica noted.

By the time they left, the girls from TSC still didn't know what would happen. The bill now sat on Governor Schwarzenegger's desk, and they couldn't be sure what he would do when he saw it. Jessica stepped outside and collapsed on the bench, exhausted. They had done everything they could. Would their efforts be enough to pass the bill? They were hopeful, but couldn't be sure. They left the Capitol, gathering their signs for the long drive home.

CHAPTER FIVE

MAKEUP ARTISTS TO THE STARS

On October 7, 2005, the California Safe Cosmetics Act was signed into law by Governor Schwarzenegger. This was a huge victory for Jessica and TSC. They had taken on the cosmetics industry and won! These teenagers (who were too young to even vote) fought hard for something they believed in and actually influenced the law and the world. You would think that would be enough, but not for Jessica. SB 484 was only the beginning.

In April 2007, TSC decided to do a "Don't Be Fooled" campaign. The project was designed to not only educate the public, but also to reach out to the companies themselves. To do that, they went to their Dirty Dozen list for help.

One professional who is studying the chemicals on the Dirty Dozen list (among others) and alerting people to their dangers is Dr. Maggie Louie, an assistant professor at Dominican University of California. Dr. Louie has said that she got involved in studying this issue because of Jessica! She now lectures about the toxic chemicals in makeup. She explains how the chemicals get absorbed into our bodies and stay in the fat tissue. Those chemicals can have a toxic effect over time—slowly poisoning our bodies.

One particularly nasty family of chemicals is called phthalates. These industrial chemicals are found in hair spray, nail polish, deodorant, gel, and countless other products. Phthalates have been associated with birth defects and can cause damage to major body organs such as your kidneys, lungs, and liver. Talc, another harmful ingredient, is a main component in eye shadow, baby powder, and soap. Talc has been linked with ovarian and lung cancer.

Check if the soap you use contains talc. If so, it may be toxic. A list of companies who sell "green" soap is available in the index.

Dr. Rebecca Sutton, a scientist at the Environmental Working Group based out of Washington, D.C., says, "We're not exposed to one chemical, our bodies absorb a soup of them every day. We don't know enough on how they affect our bodies when they interact, but we should be concerned."

GREEN INFO: Environmental Working Group researches everything from protecting our air, to protecting your pet! Their website, **www.ewg.org,** is a great source of practical information.

But people are not concerned enough. That's why TSC wanted to target the cosmetics companies themselves. If the public

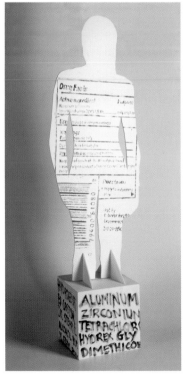

wouldn't listen, perhaps the companies would. Teens for Safe Cosmetics had nothing against these companies. In fact, they liked them. Remember, these girls joined this group because most of them really had an interest in makeup. They simply wanted to convince the companies to start turning green and produce healthier products.

The first step in the "Don't Be Fooled" campaign was to make life-size wooden cutouts of some of the most popular products on the market. Their primary goal in using the oversized product renderings was to draw attention to the companies producing ing the products. If people knew the products contained harmful chemicals and stopped using them, the companies might offer green alternatives. The second step was to hand out the Greener Alternatives lists so that the people would know which cosmetics companies truly put the health of their customers first. Unfortunately, their campaign didn't work as well as they had hoped. They got absolutely no response from the companies putting out the potentially harmful products.

Unwilling to be ignored, some members of TSC teamed up with the national Campaign for Safe Cosmetics to try a different approach. They decided to go to the professionals, hosting an event for makeup artists in Los Angeles, California. Famous makeup artists were invited to come and try green makeup alternatives, provided by Iredale Mineral Cosmetics.

If the chemicals in most popular makeup brands are harmful to people who use a small amount each day, imagine what effect they could have on those who use them *all day long*. The thought behind TSC's newest project was simple: If makeup professionals knew about the toxins in their favorite products, maybe they would influence companies to offer green alternatives. It was worth a try.

Being a Hollywood makeup artist can be a very glamorous career. Many of these makeup artists work on films and with celebrities. A good makeup artist can make someone look like an alien, a monster, or a vampire! Makeup can make an actor look older, younger, completely different, or just plain beautiful. The makeup artists have to consider many variables, such as lighting, the age of the character, and the time period of the production. Some makeup artists take their jobs to the extreme—creating prosthetic devices (like fake noses) to create a certain look. It is such an involved art form that there is now an Academy Award presented for Best Makeup.

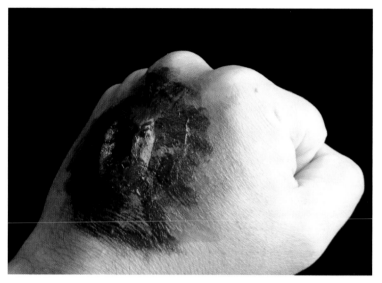

Don't worry, that's not a real gun shot wound ... it's the handiwork of a talented makeup artist.

This may sound like pure fun, but are there hazards in this exciting job? Sadly, the answer is yes. For one, these artists are assaulted by an incredible number of chemicals while doing makeup and hair for their famous clients. The hair spray, cosmetics, spray-on tans, dyes, and oils are only a few of the products they have to deal with. If the makeup we put on our bodies is potentially harmful, how does it affect the makeup artists who handle hundreds of the products every day?

Jessica asked some of the makeup artists that very question, and she was amazed by what she heard. She listened to story after story of health-related problems that these professionals believed were caused by using unsafe products on a daily basis. They consistently spoke of reproductive problems, asthma, numbness, cancer, and everything in between.

Some of the makeup artists seemed open to trying green alternatives, but most were reluctant to change their products. They are in a unique environment where the makeup they apply must stay on all day under difficult conditions. This requires very heavy makeup—and green makeup tends to be much lighter. This was a concern that many of the makeup artists voiced to Jessica.

There is some good news on the horizon, though. The popularity of high-definition television (HDTV) may change Hollywood's long-standing reliance on heavy makeup. That's because HDTV has unforgiving clarity. The incredible detail that viewers crave also shows wrinkles, pores, and other perceived imperfections.

To create the looks they want, actors must still use makeup—but if the makeup is too thick, it will show on HDTV. So, lighter makeup is starting to gain popularity. Perhaps this is the opportunity green makeup companies have been waiting for! If even one makeup artist turns green, we will be one step closer to a healthier planet. After all, if movie stars begin using green makeup, millions of people will probably follow.

As Jessica discovered, changing the mindset of people who have used certain products their entire lives is incredibly hard. Still, the event was a great success. Many of the artists Jessica spoke with at the close of the event were really excited about the green makeup they tried out that day—and a few even vowed to stop using unsafe products altogether.

The only way to truly change things, however, is for many people to demand change. If consumers continue to buy cosmetics from companies that use toxic chemicals, they are not motivating these companies to change. But if they refused to buy their products, those companies would have to consider changing. After all, for many cosmetics companies, it's all about the green—which is the color of money! If you don't give them any of your money, you will force them to turn *environmentally green.*

OPI is a good example of a major company that listened to its customers and made a change. OPI makes the most popular nail polish in the world. That is why the Campaign for Safe Cosmetics, along with Teens for Safe Cosmetics, decided to target that company. If any company was going to start turning green, TSC thought it might be OPI.

OPI had already turned green in Europe, where they no longer use toxic chemicals. This meant that the company already had the formula to eliminate toxins from their U.S. brand. The trick was getting them to see that Americans (just like Europeans) thought healthy and environmentally safe products were important.

Jessica had a personal interest in this because OPI used to be her favorite product, and she really missed using it. She desperately wanted them to eliminate the toxic chemicals (phthalates in particular) from their nail polish. But until then, she would not support the company or use their products.

In an effort to get OPI to use the same green practices they use in Europe here in the United States, TSC members went to the streets. They hung out all day at the trendy Third Street Promenade in Santa Monica, California.

The Santa Monica Pier.

The girls wanted to be sure they were noticed, so they dressed up as beauty queens. Their outfits were completed with sashes that said "Miss Treatment." This play on words was used to highlight how they believed the company was treating customers.

At first, Jessica was very embarrassed to be in public dressed in a gown and tiara while trying to get people to talk to her. Although Jessica recalls many people coming back multiple times for information, she also remembers being ignored or laughed at.

When they were not talking to people, the girls marched together and sang the chant they wrote:

1-2-3-4 … Toxic chemicals no more.
5-6-7-8 … OPI reformulate!

The media were there to capture the event, so Jessica used the opportunity to reach even more people. She spoke in front of the cameras, asking people to call OPI and tell them they would not use their products until they stopped using poisonous ingredients—and it turns out that many people did!

Although Senate Bill 484 was important because it forced companies to disclose their harmful ingredients, it sadly did nothing to stop the companies from using them. For now, it would take rallies like this to make the public aware of the problem and demand change.

Shortly after the rally, a *Los Angeles Times* reporter called OPI for a statement. With all the pressure from their customers bearing down on them, OPI said that they *did* plan to reformulate! They were removing dibutyl phthalate (DBP), the very toxic chemical Jessica had asked them to remove, from all of their products. The team at TSC had done it again!

CHAPTER SIX

THE BROWER AWARDS

In April 2006, Jessica got a phone call that changed her life. She was told that she had won a prestigious Brower Youth Award! This award is like the Oscars for young environmental activists. Jessica was honored just to be considered for the award, so when she got the call she was stunned.

Each year, the Brower Youth Award is presented to six people from ages 13 to 22. They are selected from all over North America. Brower Youth Award recipients are considered to be the leading environmental advocates in the country, passionately trying to make a difference in our world. They also possess the leadership skills and drive to make their projects successful.

The award is named after David Brower, an environmentalist who spent his life working for conservation. David was a mountain climbing enthusiast with a love of the wilderness. That love led him to become the first executive director of the Sierra Club, America's oldest and largest environmental organization. Mr. Brower was also the founder of the Earth Island Institute, an organization dedicated to promoting projects and leaders committed to the protection of our environment. The Earth Island Institute is the organization behind the Brower Youth Awards.

At first, Jessica was reluctant to apply for the award. Judi Shils had nominated her a few months back, though, so she felt she owed it to her to follow through. Jessica believed strongly in what she was doing, but she was convinced that others were doing bigger things. Just as she had doubts in confronting Governor Schwarzenegger, Jessica once again had the sense of being a small fish in a big pond.

Luckily, Judi persuaded her to go for it. Judi knew that Jessica's work was having a big impact. After all, the 17-year-old had already influenced major companies, helped to get a Senate bill passed, and educated countless people on their right to make safe and healthy choices. That was only the tip of the iceberg. Jessica

Jessica and Judi Shils at the Brower Awards ceremony.

49

was still actively working on these projects—and by receiving this award, she would be in a position to do even more.

The award ceremony was held in the historic Herbst Theatre in San Francisco. The recipients were there early, practicing their speeches and enjoying the opening events. Jessica got to see many of the current Earth Island projects, visit with the other winners, and enjoy the hip-hop entertainment. There was also plenty of food, and as you probably guessed, it was all local and organic.

After the opening reception, Jessica nervously headed to her seat. Her entire family sat in the audience, cheering Jessica on. Although she now spoke in public quite a bit, this night was different. The thought of standing up in front of the hundreds of people waiting in the massive theater to honor her was overwhelming. Jessica felt like her heart was going to jump right out of her chest. Plus, in her head, she was reliving the nightmare of falling at her school presentation. She did not want anything to go wrong on this night. Jessica did her best to push those thoughts from her head as she nervously waited for her turn to speak.

Jessica humbly listened as the winners were announced. It was very impressive. The award recipients were introduced by showing a film about each recipient and his or her project. Prior to the ceremony, a film crew from Earth Island had gone to Jessica's hometown to film her story. They even followed Jessica to Santa Monica for the OPI rally.

All the projects that these dedicated young people were involved with were amazing. The opening videos were so incredible that they elicited standing ovations from the packed auditorium.

GREEN INFO: To see Jessica's video and learn more about the Brower Youth Awards, visit www.broweryouthawards.org.

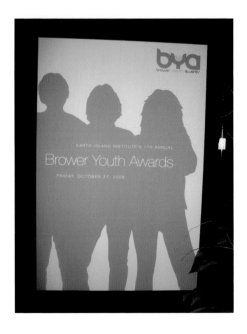

In addition to receiving recognition from other environmentalists, the winners receive a cash award of $3,000 to help them continue their work. More importantly, they each gain access to all the resources at Earth Island Institute going forward. The organization will assist in promoting their projects through research materials, publicity, and personnel. Jessica now had access to an entire environmental network!

The winners were also treated to a week of fun. They traveled together in a biodiesel bus and spoke about their projects at a number of high schools. The winners also got to go on a camping trip to beautiful Point Reyes National Park in Northern California.

Prior to this experience, Jessica's idea of camping was a hotel, and her idea of hiking was walking around the mall. On her camping trip into the great outdoors, Jessica discovered that in addition to *saving* the environment, she really enjoyed hanging out there. Jessica hiked, swam, and even ate her first s'more!

Being away from home gave Jessica a chance to bond with the other recipients. Friendships were formed that would last long after their road trip ended. Although Jessica has many friends at school, she sometimes feels like she is a little different. Her passion for working with TSC, rather than playing sports or attending high school activities, often makes her feel as if there is no one with whom she truly connects. All of that changed after she received the Brower Youth Award. Suddenly, Jessica found herself surrounded by teens who shared her passion for protecting our planet.

CHAPTER SEVEN

PROJECT PROM

There was one school activity that Jessica *was* excited about: the prom. Prom night is a big deal in high school, and Jessica wanted to use the excitement of the prom as the theme for TSC's next event. Obviously, most girls wear makeup to the prom, so showing teens how great the green alternatives could be was a natural fit.

On the day of their prom, many girls go to department stores to get makeovers. TSC decided to offer their own makeovers using only green products. This would be a great way for girls to try the makeup, and it would also be a fun type of community service.

As Jessica stated for a local newspaper, the *Marin Independent Journal*, "Teens should be able to look their best at prom without worrying about the body burden of all these chemicals."

The event grew bigger and bigger in the days leading up to the prom. In response to this, they decided to rent space in Union Square, which sits in the middle of seven major department stores in San Francisco. These were the same stores where many girls would flock to have their makeup done for prom.

TSC put up three tents in Union Square, each for a different purpose. One tent was for general information where they passed out the Dirty Dozen and Greener Alternatives fliers. A second tent, hosted by Whole Foods Market, offered a collection of skin care companies doing mini-facials, and a sampling of organic products. In the third tent, professional skin care specialists provided free makeovers using green products by Iredale Mineral Cosmetics.

There was also a big stage where a full program took place. The Bob Hill Band (winner of the earlier TSC event, Battle of the Bands) played to help draw people into the area. The girls set up about a hundred chairs so people could comfortably enjoy the music—and listen to some distinguished speakers. One of these speakers was Senator Migden, who spoke to the crowd about the importance of knowing what chemicals are in personal products.

Jessica, in pink, above and below, addresses the crowd at Union Square in San Francisco.

The speakers, the tents, and the band all drew a lot of attention, but that was nothing compared to the girls themselves. They came to the rally dressed in prom dresses, tiaras, and combat boots! Their goal was to focus attention on both the prom season and Earth Day. (The boots represented their fight against toxic chemicals.) Jessica was decked out in a pink sequined prom dress, a glittery tiara, and camouflage boots.

There were about 30 campaign members dressed like that, so they drew quite a crowd wherever they went. One of their primary goals in selecting the location near the department stores was to educate the makeup artists who worked there. They hoped that many of these makeup artists would drop by and try out some of the green products. TSC knew that if the public demanded safer products, the companies would change—and that demand could get a kick start from the makeup pros.

Unfortunately, safe cosmetics can be hard to find in many places. They can also be expensive. Over time, with more people requesting them (and more professional makeup artists using them), they will become more readily available and affordable.

The 30 TSC crusaders, armed with signs and information, marched into the department stores to spread their message. They weren't being unreasonable with the stores or the cosmetics companies. They were only asking them to start turning green. They knew it would be unrealistic to expect major changes all at once. For today, their goal was simply to convince each store to offer at least one organic product line.

Jessica led the group as they wove single-file through the aisles of the first store. They looked like a giant, colorful snake. It was designed to be a peaceful rally, so the girls were pretty quiet. All they did was hand letters to the workers, which asked them to please offer at least one organic alternative.

It was all going great until Jessica looked up and saw a manager heading her way. He was talking into a walkie-talkie and did not look happy. The girls were very visible (which was exactly what they had intended), but that was apparently bad for business. So, the girls were kicked out of the store!

This was a first for most of the girls, and it was very disturbing. Jessica had never been in trouble before. To have people tell her she wasn't welcome was very upsetting. However, that did not discourage her from leading the girls to six other stores. Some of the stores welcomed them, but several of them also asked the girls to leave. When they had been to all the major stores, they marched back outside, and Jessica led the girls in a chant:

1 – 2 – 3 – 4 ... Toxic chemicals no more!
5 – 6 – 7 – 8 ... FDA must regulate!

The day ended up being a huge success. The message was heard by many people. Since that rally, Barneys New York and Macy's have integrated green products into both their cosmetics departments and their clothing departments! Many other department stores are following this growing trend. It all starts with people willing to voice their opinion and stand up for what is right. Once again, a few young girls helped to create big change. They also managed to create some unintended entertainment that day.

A very strange and random thing happened just as the rally was winding down. When TSC member Erin Schrode (Judi Shils' daughter) agreed to participate in the rally, she anticipated that the most strenuous thing she would be doing was carrying a sign and speaking to the crowd. However, in the middle of the event, after hearing the music stop, she looked over and saw three young men running off with the laptop that had been powering the sound.

"I wasn't going to let them get away," Erin says. "Something in me just said: 'You're going to catch them.'" With that thought in mind, she started running after the boys. You can only imagine the looks on the faces of the crowd as Erin—dressed in a prom dress, combat boots, and a tiara—ran after the thieves through the city.

The race lasted several blocks. The bizarre scene unfolded like something out of a movie. People were cheering Erin on as she dodged cars and raced through the heart of San Francisco. As she ran, Erin yelled for people to stop the thieves, but in the end, it was Erin who caught one of them.

The police quickly arrived to help, and Erin was able to lead them to the second suspect, who was apprehended. The third suspect got away. Unfortunately, they did not recover the laptop, but they did find a stolen purse and some cash. Erin's speed and bravery were credited with saving the day. The headline in the *Marin Independent Journal* read: **FASHION POLICE: Marin teen chases down thieves in S.F. while clad in prom dress, combat boots.**

After that episode, Erin was asked to be on The Tonight Show with Jay Leno and the national Fox News Channel! It was a bizarre ending to the otherwise peaceful—and successful—rally.

CHAPTER EIGHT

A BRIGHT GREEN FUTURE

Teens for Safe Cosmetics continues to grow and organize activities each month. Jessica's hope is that someday soon, they will be able to say that all toxic chemicals are banned in the United States. Their first priority is makeup. But since these ingredients are found in many other things, such as water bottles, clothing dyes, and purse linings, they will continue to educate the public with the hope of forcing companies to use safer ingredients in *all* products.

In the meantime, TSC is taking matters into their own hands. Jessica and several other campaign members recently worked with one of their partner companies, EO (Essential Oil), to make their own line of perfume. The girls were given an array of oils, which they mixed in different ways to create a scent that they thought teens would like. They created a fragrance that they all loved. They called it "I." When the teens were trying to think of a name that would best describe their campaign, they came up with adjectives like innovative, inspiring, and irresistible. "I" was a short version of all those words.

This perfume is sold in sustainable packaging, so it is as green as it can be. TSC sells the perfume at their events, and the money is used to support their campaign. This line has evolved into a partnership with Whole Foods Market called "Teens Turning Green." They are hoping to launch a complete line of green products for teens by the fall of 2009.

Jessica has enjoyed every aspect of working with TSC, and although she hopes to continue to be involved, she is also ready to step outside her comfort zone once again. If you had asked Jessica two years ago what her plans were after high school, she would have said that she was going to stay close to home and attend a local college. But now, with college applications scattered across her desk, Jessica feels the need to go a bit farther, to explore the world from another view. Jessica's new path may take her as far as our nation's capital, Washington, D.C.

Jessica plans to study law, with the hope of working in public health. She feels that with her passion to make the world a safer place, this avenue would allow her to have the most impact. Her experiences with TSC, and her exposure to the legislative process in California, have made her see that sometimes changing the law is the best way to get people to do what's right.

A good example of this is solar heating. (Solar heating converts the sun's power into heat for things like hot water and heated swimming pools.) Everyone agrees that solar heat can save both energy and money, but how many people have actually switched over to it? Well, Hawaii lawmakers, like Jessica, realize that sometimes people need help to do the right thing. Hawaii recently became the first state to pass a law requiring all new homes (starting in 2010) to have a solar water heater.

The sun is an incredible source of energy. The solar panels in the picture above help convert the suns rays into energy we can use.

Jeff Mikulina, director of the Sierra Club in Hawaii, says, "This is a landmark measure that is really going to get us closer to a clean energy future." Hawaii is taking a step toward turning green. And remember, that's all it takes—one step at a time. Think of the energy we'd save if every state took this measure!

Regardless of where Jessica decides to go to college, one thing is for sure: We have not heard the last of her. Jessica says, "I plan on continuing to teach people and tell them that if they do not like something about the world, whether it be the fact that there are possible carcinogens [cancer-causing substances] in personal care products or something completely different, it is their responsibility to work toward change. ... I want people to know that regardless of age, we must start now to sustain the world for future generations. We have all the resources and technology; all we need is people to initiate the use of environmentally safe products and practices." You don't have to turn green overnight. Begin with something that you can do now.

When Jessica is asked why she got involved in Teens for Safe Cosmetics, she says, "It was an easy place for me to start. Using safer makeup affects you on such a personal level. I could go home and immediately make a difference." You can make a difference, too.

GREEN TIPS: For starters, recycle everything you can. It is estimated that 85 percent of what we throw away can be reused. Did you know that it takes 20 times more energy to make aluminum cans from scratch than from recycled ones? Think about the energy you could save the next time you toss your can in the trash.

Turn out the lights! When you leave a room, make sure everything is off. If you need to use lights, be sure they are compact fluorescent bulbs. Ask your parents what type of light bulbs are used in your house. Compact fluorescent bulbs use about 65 percent less energy than regular ones—and they provide the same light at about the same cost.

The environmentally friendly companct fluorescent bulb. Replace all your old light bulbs with these "green" bulbs!

You can also conserve water by taking shorter showers and making sure the faucets are completely turned off.

You can help reduce pollution by riding your bike more often. Cars contribute more than one-third of all the greenhouse gas emissions we produce! So when you're old enough to buy a car, buy a hybrid. Gas-guzzling SUVs can produce as much as 95,000 pounds of global-warming pollution in just one year!

Using safe makeup and personal care products should also be at the top of your list. It's up to you to take care of yourself, and to do your part in taking care of our planet. Organic products help both you and the environment. Every time you use organic products, you are taking one more step toward improving your world.

There are many more things that you can do. If you visit www.ecologue.com, you can find countless other ways to get involved in the fight to save planet Earth. What you do matters. Jessica has shown us that teens *can* make a difference.

When the California Safe Cosmetics Act passed, Jessica discovered that she could truly affect the world. She says, "Seeing the law passed was very fulfilling. I learned that I can make a difference. All it takes is confidence and belief in the cause. I never believed that teenagers, who lack the legal rights of adults and the power to vote, could have such an impact. But now I see that age is just a number, and teens have as much power to create change as adults. Sometimes, maybe more. … We cannot just let frustrating environmental issues pass us by. We are the future, and we have all the tools for improvement. Everyone has the power to make change."

Jessica Assaf acted on those words, and you can, too! In fact, you *must*. Our planet is at risk, and it is up to all of us to make our future happy and healthy. Living green is not just a new fad, but a new way of life—and it all starts with you. **So how are you going to turn the world green again?**

THE DIRTY DOZEN +

(Source: Teens for Safe Cosmetics)

The following is a list of potentially harmful chemicals to look for in your personal care products. If you see these chemicals, beware!

Butyl Acetate
Butylated Hydroxytoluene
Coal Tar
Cocamide DEA/Lauramide DEA
Diazolidinyl Urea
Ethyl Acetate
Formaldehyde
Parabens (methyl, ethyl, propyl and butyl)
Petrolatum
Phthalates
Propylene Glycol
Sodium Laureth/Sodium Laurel Sulfate
Talc
Toluene
Triethanolamine

GREENER ALTERNATIVES
(Source: Teens for Safe Cosmetics)

This is a list of companies making safer products. Check their websites and in your community, check out Whole Foods Market, Pharmaca, Good Earth, Elephant Pharmacy, and all of the local businesses who stock healthy alternatives.

ALAFFIA - alaffia.com, Hair, skin, lip and body care, soap
ASTARA - astaraskincare.com, Skin and body care. AURA
CACIA - auracacia.com, Body care, bath, essential oils,
perfume
BENEDETTA - benedetta.com, Skin and body care, soap,
deodorant, hand sanitizer
BURT'S BEES - burtsbees.com, Hair, skin, lip and body care,
soap, deodorant, makeup, sunscreen, insect repellent
CORAL WHITE - coral-cure.com/coral-white-toothpaste.htm,
Toothpaste, mouthwash
DR. BRONNER'S - drbronner.com, Body and lip care, soap
DR. HAUSCHKA - drhauschka.com, Hair, skin, lip and body
care, deodorant, makeup, sunscreen
DROPWISE ESSENTIALS - dropwise.com, Body and lip care
EARTHBOUND ORGANICS - www.earthbound.co.uk, Skin
and body care, soap
ECO LANI - ecolani.com, Sunscreen
EDEN'S KISS - edenskiss.com, Body care, bath, anti-aging
products
EO PRODUCTS - eoproducts.com, Hair, skin, lip and body
care, bath, essential oils, hand sanitizer
EVAN HEALY - evanhealy.com, Skin and body care
GRATEFUL BODY - gratefulbody.com, Skin and body care
GREEN PEOPLE - greenpeople.com, Hair, skin, lip, and body
care, deodorant, toothpaste, sunscreen
HERBAN COWBOY - herbancowboy.com, Shaving cream,
soap, deodorant
HONEYBEE GARDENS - honeybeegardens.com, Lip and
nail care, makeup
IREDALE MINERAL COSMETICS - janeiredale.com,
Makeup
JA NENE - anointyourself.com, Skin and lip care, bath
JASON - jason-natural.com, Hair, skin, and body care, de-
odorant, toothpaste, sunscreen, soap
JOSIE MARAN - josiemarancosmetics.com, Makeup

JOHN MASTERS ORGANICS - johnmasters.com, Hair, skin, lip and body care, soap
JP DURGA - jpdurga.com, Hair, skin, lip and body care, soap
JUICE BEAUTY - juicebeauty.com, Skin and lip care
JURLIQUE - jurlique.com, Skin, lip and body care, soap, bath, makeup remover
KEYS - keys-soap.com, Skin, body and hair care, insect repellent, sunscreen
LAFE'S - lafes.com, Deodorant, foot spray
LOGONA - logona.co.uk, Hair, skin and body care, toothpaste, makeup
LAVERA - lavera.com, Hair, skin, lip and body care, makeup
MIESSENCE - miessenceproducts.com, Hair, skin and body care, makeup
MOOM - imoom.com, Body care
MYCHELLE - mychelleusa.com, Skin, lip and body care
NATRACARE - natracare.com, Feminine hygiene, organic cotton wipes
NUDE SKINCARE - nudeskincare.com, Makeup
ORGANIC APOTEKE - organicapoteke.com, Skin and body care, soap, perfume
PANGEA ORGANICS - pangeaorganics.com, Skin and body care, soap
PHARMACOPIA - pharmacopia.net, Body and lip care
POMEGA5 - pomega5.com, Skin and body care
RIVER SOAP - riversoap.com, Soap and bath
SIMPLY ORGANIC - simplyorganicbeauty.com, Hair, skin and body care
SPIRIT OF BEAUTY -nutritionskincare.com, Skin and lip care
SUKI - sukipure.com, Hair, skin, lip and body care, makeup
TWEEN BEAUTY - tweenbeauty.com, Hair and lip care
WELEDA - usa.weleda.com, Hair, skin and body care, toothpaste
ZUZU - gabrielcosmeticsinc.com, Makeup